The SCIENCE BEHIND the ATHLETE

HOCKEY

India James

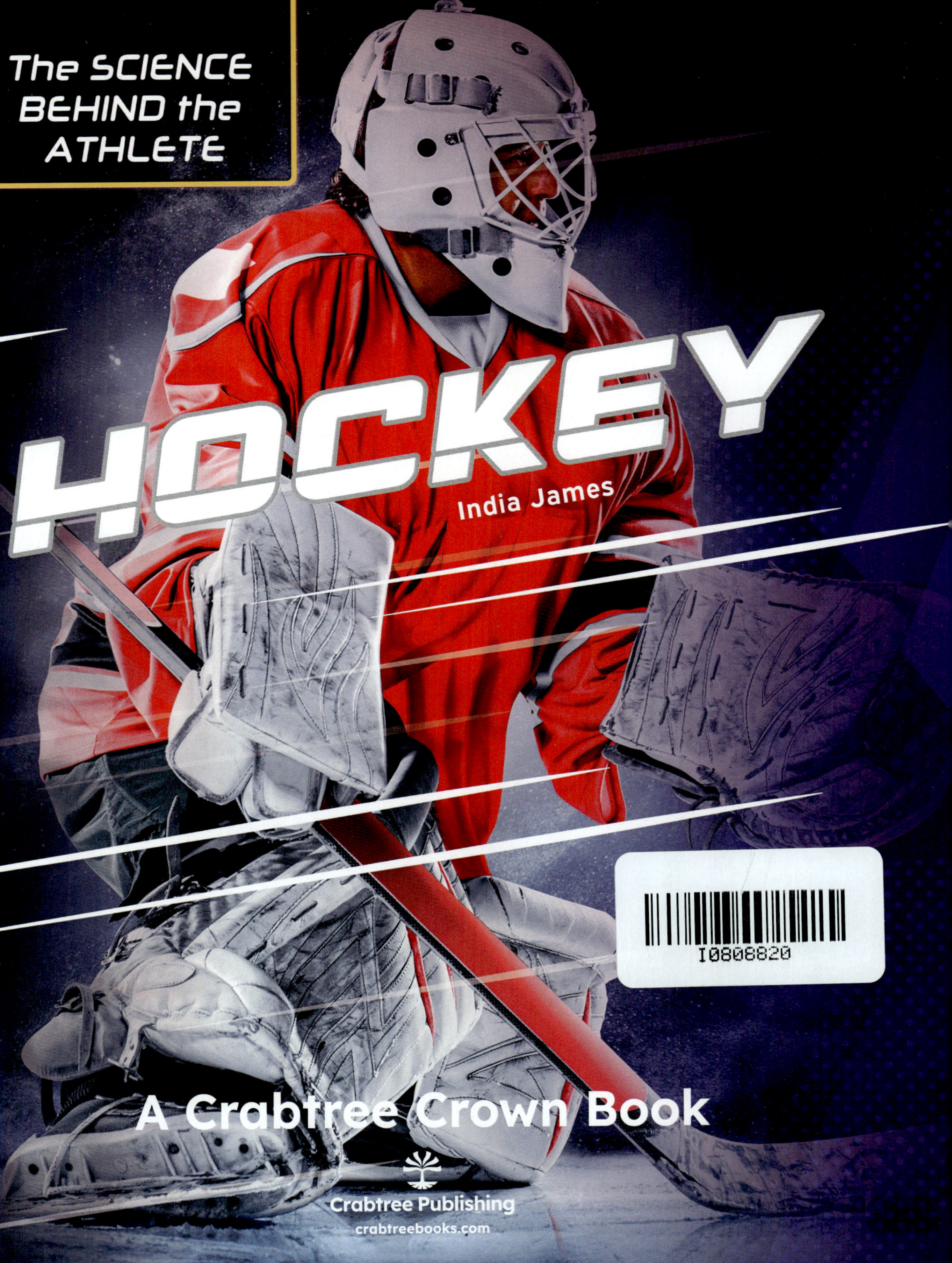

A Crabtree Crown Book

Crabtree Publishing
crabtreebooks.com

School-to-Home Support for Caregivers and Teachers

This appealing book is designed to teach students about core subject areas. Students will build upon what they already know about the subject, and engage in topics that they want to learn more about. Here are a few guiding questions to help readers build their comprehensions skills. Possible answers appear here in red.

Before Reading:

What do I know about hockey?

- *I know hockey is a sport.*
- *I know hockey is played on ice.*

What do I want to learn about this topic?

- *I want to know what the first hockey sticks were made of.*
- *I want to learn how hockey uses technology.*

During Reading:

I'm curious to know...

- *I'm curious to know how hockey sticks are made.*
- *I'm curious to know why goalies have so much equipment.*

How is this like something I already know?

- *I know hockey sticks are made of different materials.*
- *I know goalies wear pads.*

After Reading:

What was the author trying to teach me?

- *The author was trying to teach me how technology is used to help players train.*
- *The author was trying to teach me how math is used in hockey.*

How did the photographs and captions help me understand more?

- *The photographs helped me understand how science has improved hockey.*
- *The captions gave me extra information about the history of hockey.*

TABLE OF CONTENTS

WHAT IS HOCKEY?

Hockey is a sport played on ice. There are usually six players from each team on the ice at a time. Players compete to get a **puck** into the opposing team's net.

HOCKEY HOT TIP

A hockey puck is a disk that is 1 inch (2.5 cm) thick by 3 inches (7.6 cm) in diameter. It is made from a type of hardened rubber.

1 SKATES

Ice skates have been around for more than 5,000 years. The first skates were made from animal bones.

Bone skates on display at the Museum of London. People would fit the shinbones of cattle to their feet.

Ice skates work by decreasing **friction** between the skater and the ice. Animal bones were good for this, but they didn't allow the skater to turn very well.

HOCKEY HOT TIP

The first ice skates are believed to have been developed in Finland around 5,000 years ago. That's even before the great pyramids were built in Egypt!

MOVING TO METAL

In the 1400s, people in the Netherlands began skating on an iron blade attached to a piece of wood. These skates didn't slide as well as animal bones, but the iron blades allowed the skater to turn. Skaters discovered that they could go faster when a double edge was sharpened onto the blade. By the 1500s, double-bladed skates were helping people go fast on ice.

BOOTS

For most of skating history, ice skates were strapped onto shoes. Boots with a permanently attached blade weren't commonly used until the early 1900s.

HOCKEY HOT TIP

A popular hockey skate company is CCM. This company began producing hockey skates in 1905. The name comes from Canadian Cycle & Motor Company—their first skates were made with metal left over from producing cars and bicycles.

PLASTIC BOOTS

As more people started to play hockey, specific skates were developed for the sport. Plastic boots were first invented in the 1970s. These boots made the skater lean forward. This position helped the players to skate faster.

Players liked skating fast, but the plastic boot was heavy. Since the 1970s, **engineers** have developed materials to help make hockey skates lighter. The new materials aren't as heavy, but they still hold a player's ankles in the best position for speed.

2 HOCKEY STICKS

Hockey players use a hockey **stick** to push and shoot the puck down the ice. A strong stick that can control the puck is necessary for each player.

EARLY HOCKEY STICKS

The first hockey sticks were created by the Mi'kmaq, a **First Nations people** of Canada. They carved these sticks from birch and hornbeam trees. Maple became more commonly used as the sport spread across North America.

Mi'kmaq carvers are seen here making hockey sticks from hornbeam trees in Nova Scotia around 1890.

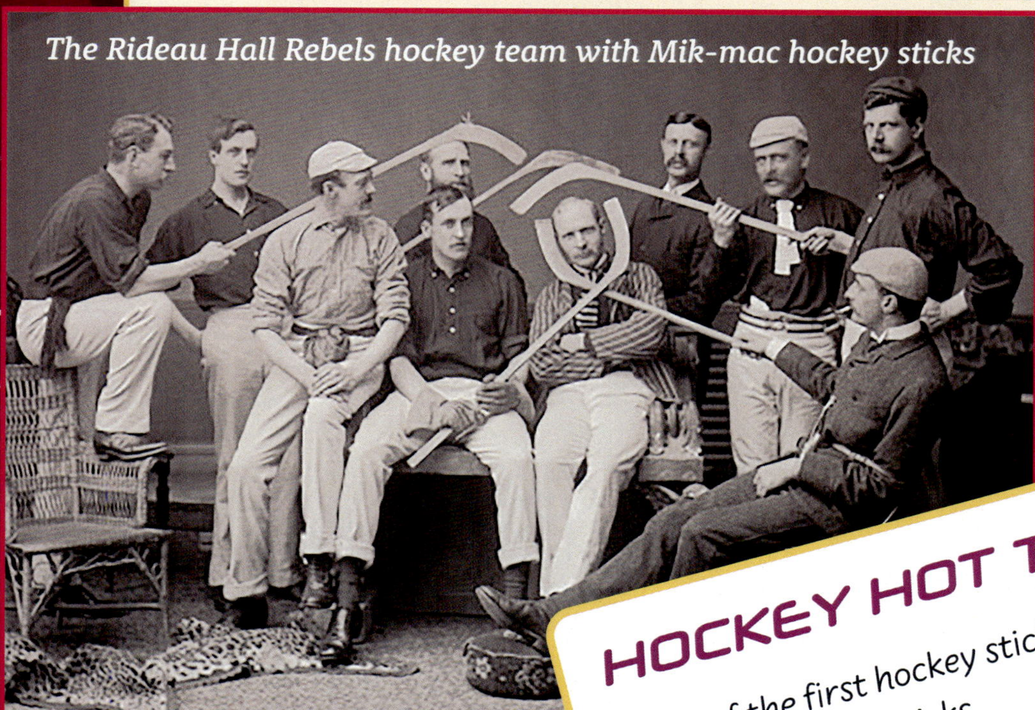

The Rideau Hall Rebels hockey team with Mik-mac hockey sticks

HOCKEY HOT TIP

Some of the first hockey sticks were called "Mik-mac" sticks.

STICK MATERIALS

Hockey sticks today are less commonly made of wood. Instead, they are often made from a **composite** of fiberglass, carbon fiber, and a strong material called Kevlar. These materials help the stick be lighter, stronger, and more flexible.

Kevlar

BLADE SHAPE

The blade is the part of the hockey stick that comes in contact with the puck. The first hockey sticks had a flat blade. Hockey players used a flat blade until the 1960s.

According to hockey legend, the first curved blade was created when a hockey stick broke during practice. The player with the broken stick decided to keep playing. He found that the broken blade worked better for controlling the puck. He decided to experiment with different types of curves in the blade. Soon, other players were using curved blades as well.

HOCKEY HOT TIP

Players called the first hockey sticks with curved blades "banana blades."

3 GOALIE EQUIPMENT

The goalie stops hockey pucks from going into the net. They stop the other team from scoring. Goalies use their sticks, their gloves, and even their bodies to prevent the other team from scoring points.

DESIGNS FROM OTHER SPORTS

Early goalie equipment came from other sports. Many goalies used baseball mitts. They added padding to the mitt to help cushion the blow of a hockey puck. Goalies also used chest protectors designed like the ones baseball catchers used.

This scene from the 1950 movie The Jackie Robinson Story *shows the equipment worn by baseball catchers at the time.*

The first leg pads were borrowed from a design used in cricket. These leg pads were often made of leather and stuffed with materials such as horsehair.

GOALIE STICKS

During the first National League Hockey (NHL) games, goalies used the same sticks as the rest of the players. Goalies soon found that a wider stick allowed them to block more shots. Now large sticks help a goalie keep the puck out of the net.

GOALIE MASKS

Goalie masks were first brought into the game in the 1950s. They help protect the player's head and face from the pucks that come flying at the net.

HOCKEY HOT TIP

Goalies often decorate their masks and helmets. Gerry "Cheesy" Cheevers, who played for the Boston Bruins, painted stitches on his mask wherever he was hit by a shot.

DESIGN WITH COMPUTERS

Today, computer technology helps goalies individually fit their gear. Materials such as plastic, foam, Kevlar, and titanium are used to shield and cushion each goalie.

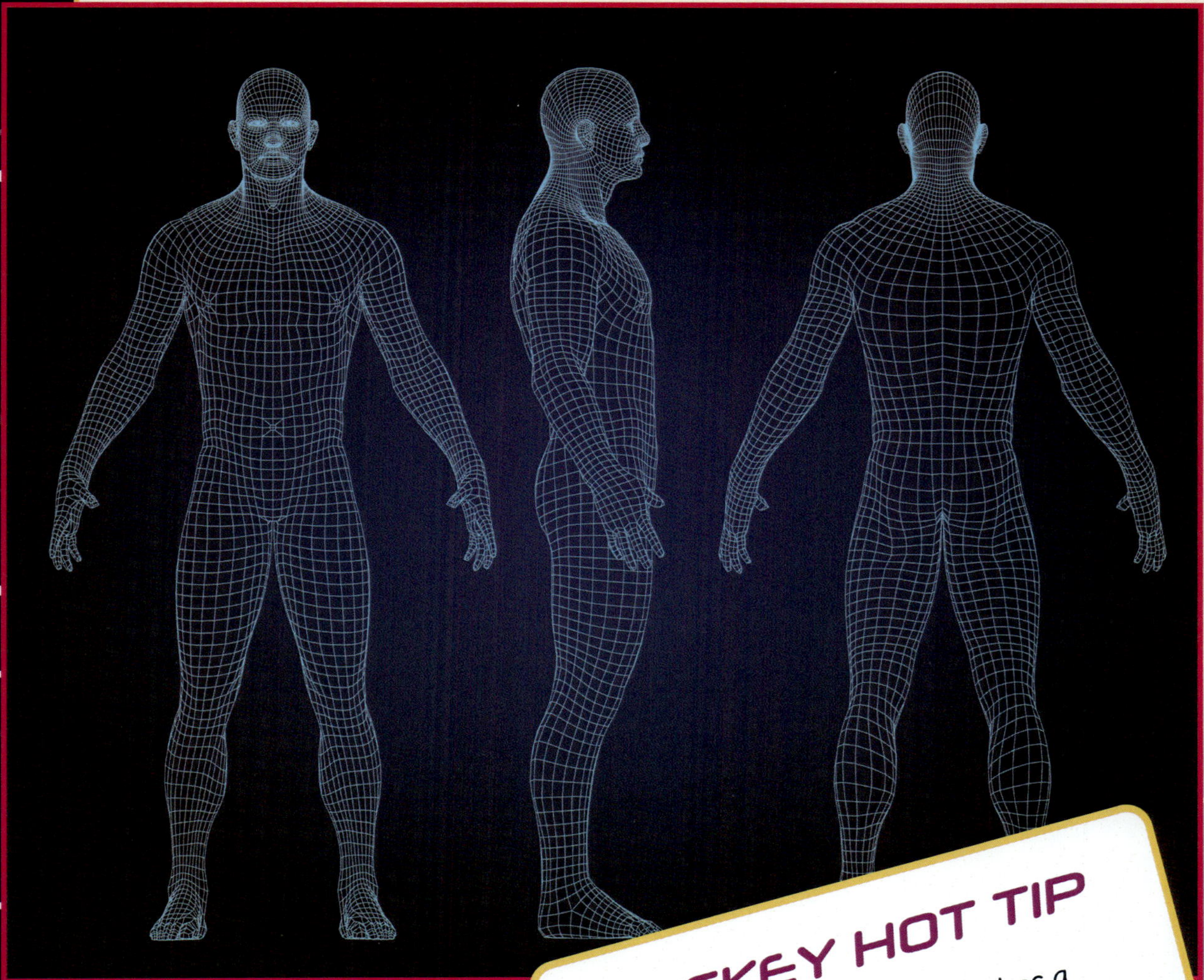

HOCKEY HOT TIP

3-D mapping technology takes a scan of each goalie's body. Pads can be made according to these precise measurements and are specific to each player.

4 TECHNOLOGY

Tracking the puck and the players are important parts of knowing how a game is going. Technology has changed the way that coaches, scouts, and spectators understand what is happening in a game.

SENSORS

NHL hockey pucks are now equipped with **sensors**. **Microchips** and other sensors are used to track the puck. The jerseys that NHL hockey players wear also have **infrared** sensors that follow each player. From this information, computers can calculate how fast the players and the puck are moving. They can also calculate how hard the puck is hit.

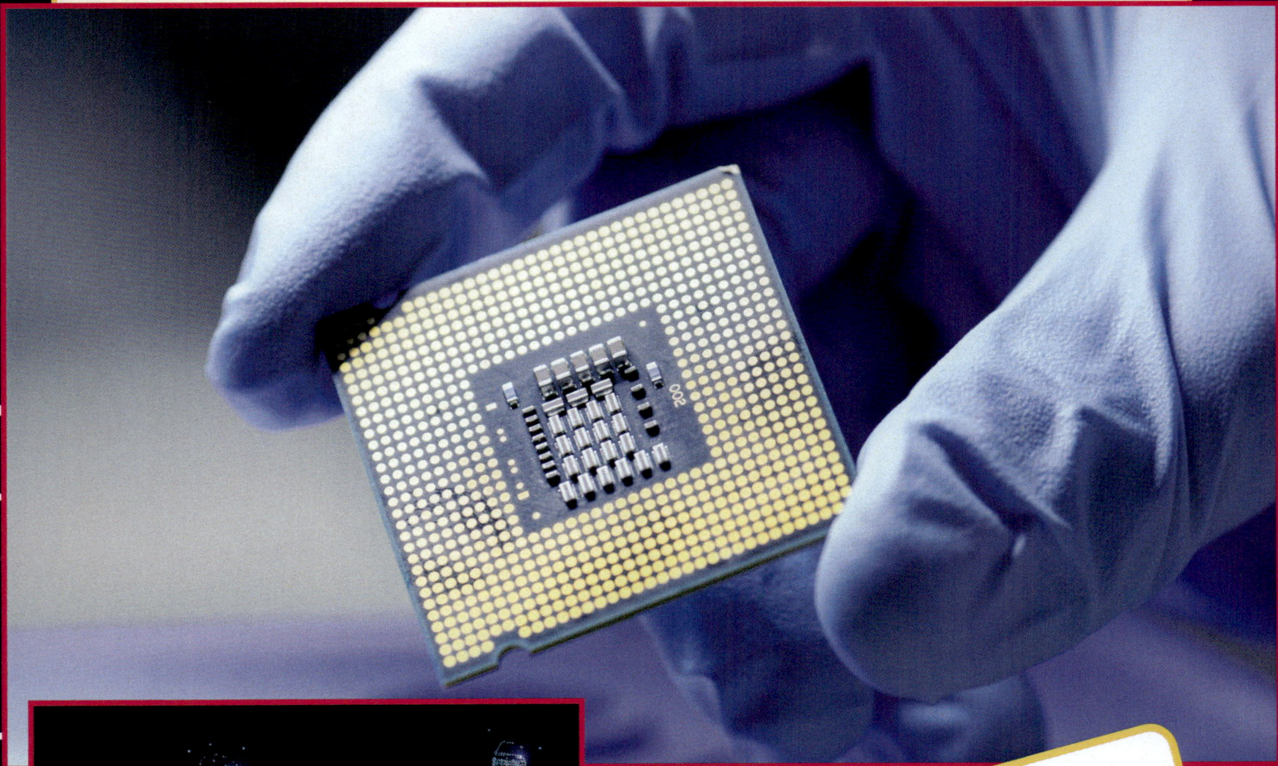

HOCKEY HOT TIP

This new system of sensors that the NHL is using can track players at a rate of 200 times per second and pucks at 2,000 times per second.

TECHNOLOGY TROUBLE

The transition to using new technology hasn't been easy. At first, the new pucks with the sensors didn't move as well on the ice as the original pucks without sensors. Scientists and engineers kept working to make the technology better. Today, players, pucks, and even the ice on which they skate can be all outfitted with state-of-the art sensors.

HOCKEY HOT TIP

The area behind the goalie is one of the most-covered areas for new sensors because so much action takes place there.

5 STATISTICS

Shots and plays might be the most exciting parts of the game, but hockey is a sport that depends a lot on math. **Statistics** is one area where math is used to help understand the game.

STATISTICS

Statistics is an area of math that collects, organizes, and **analyzes** sets of numbers. In hockey, statistics are used to explain how players are performing and how the team is doing overall. Coaches, scouts, and the media all use statistics to understand how players and teams are performing.

HOCKEY HOT TIP

Wayne Gretzky has scored the most goals in NHL history. During his 20 seasons with the NHL he scored 894 goals.

CORSI

Sometimes statistics are used to describe how the players are working together as a team. Corsi is the sum of all shots taken toward the net by players on a team, whether a shot is a goal or not. This shows how players are working together to try and score points.

FENWICK

Fenwick is a statistic very similar to Corsi. Fenwick is the total of all shots taken, but without including the number of blocked shots. Some **statisticians** use more complicated ways to calculate Fenwick too. Like Corsi, Fenwick also describes how players are working together to try and score points.

EXPECTED GOALS

Expected goals is a statistic used to predict how likely a team or player is to score a point. This is a complicated measure that is calculated by a computer.

CONCLUSION

Hockey is an exciting game. The sticks, pucks, and skates have changed since the first time hockey was played. Science and technology can help make the sport more exciting and safer in the future.

GLOSSARY

analyze (AN-uh-lize): To examine carefully and in detail

composite (kuhm-POZ-it): Made of two or more materials

engineer (en-juh-NEER): A person who is trained in the use of math, science, and creative thinking to design things that solve problems and meet needs

First Nations people (furst NEY-shuhnz PEE-puhl): The first inhabitants of Canada

friction (FRIK-shuhn): A force that is created when one object rubs against another

infrared (in-fruh-RED): Producing or using rays of light that are invisible to human eyes

microchip (MAHY-kroh-chip): A tiny piece of material containing electronic circuits that allow it to store a lot of information

puck (pukh): A small, hard disk made of rubber that is used in hockey

sensor (SEN-ser): An electronic device that measures and monitors conditions from its environment

statistician (stat-i-STISH-uhn): A person who collects and studies statistics

statistics (stuh-TIS-tiks): A branch of math that collects, organizes, and analyzes numbers

stick (stik): A long-handled stick with a curve at one end that hockey players use to hit a puck

INDEX

COMPREHENSION QUESTIONS

1. When were the first ice skates developed?
   a. 6,000 years ago
   b. 5,000 years ago
   c. 4,000 years ago
2. Which technology is used in hockey pucks?
   a. microchips
   b. microwaves
   c. X-rays
3. What is an example of a statistic measured in hockey?
   a. jump height
   b. timed 100-yard dash
   c. Corsi
4. **True or False:** Math is important in hockey.
5. **True or False:** Hockey stick blades have always been the same shape.

Answers: 1. B, 2. A, 3. C, 4. True, 5. False

ABOUT THE AUTHOR

India James writes about science, technology, and math for young readers. She loves when science comes together with sports. India lives in Ohio with her family.

Written by: India James
Designed by: Kathy Walsh
Series Development: James Earley
Proofreader: Melissa Boyce
Educational Consultant: Marie Lemke M.Ed.

Photographs: Shutterstock; Cover & Title pg: Eugene Onischenki, Lilo Alfonso, geen graphy, your; p 2-31 backgrounds: Lilo Alfonso, your; pg numbers: Aleksandr Sulga; p 4: David InderliedviaNewscom, Duisty Cline; p 5 @Wiki, zelenal; p 6 anpsports095780/Newscom]; p 7: Jan-Willem Kunnen; P 8: @Wiki, Krasowit; p 9: @flickr; p 10: Za BonDurant/Icon Sportswire, Joel MarklundviaNewscom; p 11: Frank Jansky/Icon SportswireviaNewscom; p 12: @Wiki; p 13: Frank Jansky/Icon Sportswire, Composite_Carbonman; p 14: McKinnon Kyle; p 15: Lennart M-Ansson; p 16: Scott Hasse; p 17: Library of Congress; p 18: @flickr; p 19: Scott Hasse; p 20: Mark LoMoglio/Icon SMI; p 21: Ovocim; p 22: Joel Marklund; p 23: Gorodenkoff, Maxim Gaigul p24: Jeanine Leech/Icon SMIviaNewscom; p 25: Michael Stuparyk; p 26: David KirouacviaNewscom; p 27: Duncan WilliamsviaNewscom; p 28: ViDI Studio; p 29: Michael Tureski/Icon SMI

Crabtree Publishing

crabtreebooks.com 800-387-7650

Printed in Canada/012024/CP20231127

Published in Canada
Crabtree Publishing
616 Welland Ave.
St. Catharines, Ontario
L2M 5V6

Published in the United States
Crabtree Publishing
347 Fifth Ave
Suite 1402-145
New York, NY 10016

Library and Archives Canada Cataloguing in Publication
Available at Library and Archives Canada

Library of Congress Cataloging-in-Publication Data
Available at the Library of Congress

Hardcover: 978-1-0398-3895-6
Paperback: 978-1-0398-3980-9
Ebook (pdf): 978-1-0398-4054-6
Epub: 978-1-0398-4126-0